Hurtz

Jasmine Gardosi

VERVE
POETRY PRESS
BIRMINGHAM

PUBLISHED BY VERVE POETRY PRESS
Birmingham, West Midlands, UK
www.vervepoetrypress.com
mail@vervepoetrypress.com

FIRST PUBLISHED MAY 2019

Printed in Birmingham by Positive Print

ISBN: 978-1-912565-22-1

Recent studies have shown that cutting your thumb chopping kale hurts more than when chopping bacon, because you are about to eat kale and not bacon.

Having your foot run over by your Ford Focus is equivalent to pain acquired when a 26-year-old blonde rejects you for your wingman.

And contrary to the popular saying, the pain of an ant is *not* equal to that of a giant. An ant losing a leg would equate to a friendly punch on a human shoulder. Two legs, if the punch is passive aggressive.

Once the International Hurtz Scale is programmed into glasses and contact lenses, you'll be able to see your pain. Not just feel it.

red *#ff0000*	*10 hrtz*
orange *#ffa500*	*20 hrtz*
yellow *#ffff00*	*30 hrtz*
green *#008000*	*40 hrtz*
turquoise *#40e0d0*	*50 hrtz*
blue *#0000ff*	*60 hrtz*
candy pink *#e4717a*	*hang on*
raspberry glace *#915f6d*	*are you sure*
indigo *#4b0082*	*okay*
violet *#7f00ff*	*100 hrtz*
purple *#800080*	*110 hrtz*

grey
#808080

120 hrtz

black
#000000

130 hrtz

brown
#964b00

140 hrtz

orange
#ffa500

but we

red
#ff0000

we've already had

white
#ffffff

170 hrtz

flamingo
#fc8eac

oh, come on

pistachio
#93c572

Clive

shimmering blush
#d98695

did you do this?

outrageous orange
#ff6e4a

goddamnit, Clive

For reference 1.0

Headache is equal to
bust lip

Foot cramp is equal to
grazed knee

Standing on piece of Lego
is two times walking into window
[though walking into window is worth 0.25
more when window is in public]

Dropping phone in toilet
is equivalent to slamming hand
in car door

Self-blame accumulated by burning tongue on
noodle soup so you can't taste the rest of it
is 3.5 times that of losing biscuit in tea

Sense of loss when friend
takes disproportionately large lick
of *your* ice cream is only half
of watching Mufasa death scene

Missing bus by ten seconds
is greater than or equal to regret
of sleeping with bra on

Signing off a text to your boss with a kiss
is equivalent to doing a poo before you realise
there's no loo roll;

there's no going back

Pain scientist

Observation 15
Halls of residence. Burn own arm on baking tray. *Pewf.* Purple cloud. As predicted. Forgot notepad. Will make note of correct hypothesis once notepad acquired from bedroom. Will make note to not forget notepad.

Observation 303
Housemates shout 'Surprise!' on entry to flat. Stub toe on doorframe. Magenta. *[Fascinating. Never known pain like this!]* Follow magenta through fog of poppers. Difficult because of fog of poppers. Jot calculation on inside of party hat. On brink of groundbreaking new formula.

Observation 785
Can actually tell what grade each classmate has received for dissertation, *[right down to the exact percentage!]* by shade of orange issued as each classmate stares at paper and lowers it slowly.

Observation 1,002
New lab. Know who not to ask for coffee based on colleagues' morning shade of blue *[more accurate each day! Tomorrow will get perfect].*

Observation 1,231
Propose to Elodie. Push ring up finger. Too small. Perceive that Elodie's higher level of joy neutralises minor tint of red. Momentous discovery.

Observation 13,409
Billy now 3 yrs 8 mos. Burns own arm on candle. *Pewf.* Purple cloud. As predicted. Did not forget notepad.

Burgundy

I got my diagnosis.
I have burgundy.

It's a relief to know.
I'm not weak or lazy.
I have burgundy.

When people ask how I am today,
I tell them I have burgundy.
Sometimes I feel fine, but I know —
deep down — I have burgundy.

Burgundy goes with all of my clothes.

Nathan also has burgundy.
He takes Typtamine
for his burgundy.
I take Typtamine
for my burgundy, too.

Sarah says she has burgundy
but she drinks a lot and I don't.
I wonder at what stage of the burgundy
this will happen.

A friend of a friend had burgundy
but he took different tablets
to the ones my doctor gave me.
And then he stopped taking them.

And then he died,
and that makes me think,
will I die too, because I'm not
taking the tablets he took
to stop him being so burgundy?

Nathan's doctor was wrong.
He is not burgundy.
He actually has carmine.
They have started him
on Dozapram.

The Morrisons lady gave me
the wrong change and I cried,
probably because I have burgundy.

I saw a job I might really like,
but I don't think I'll apply,
because I have burgundy.

I have to stay in the bathroom
for a very long time when I see
my ex laughing with someone,
probably because I am burgundy.

I think burgundy
is my favourite colour.

Bisque *#ffe4c4*

We kindly remind you that you are permitted to feel any colour. Any colour. Apart from *this* one. You may feel the colour that makes you flick the light switch fifty-four times before you sleep. You may feel the colour that makes you shout over Christmas dinner at your mother. You may feel the colour that makes you talk to yourself on the bus home. You may feel the colour that makes you quit your job to take a coach to Manchester, say, and sit on a bench for five hours. You may feel the colour that makes you slap your forehead against the bricks of your neighbour's house as you take the bins in. You may feel ivory. You may feel snow. You may feel floralwhite. You may feel blanchedalmond. We don't mind.

But should you feel *this* colour, please understand that we will abseil in through your window. We will dismantle your lock, or we will kick down your door. We will pin you to the floor. We will make you pack your bags. We will call your next of kin. We will assign you a bed. And when we release you, remember, please do not feel this colour.

The selection of colours you may feel is wide-ranging. Never feel like you have no options. Enjoy your life. Feel green. Feel orange. Feel purple, as you corner your wife in your bedroom. Feel tan, as the Year 9s lock you in the cubicle. Go live in underground dens and wallow in mustard yellow. Walk chest-first into bar fights. Disappear from your tutorials. Cut your scalp in the bathroom mirror. Push the pedal down to 110 mph — by accident. We don't mind. It's okay. Just don't feel this one. Don't feel it. Don't feel it. It is not permitted.

We appreciate you trying. Because you do. You really do. You buy plane tickets to hot countries. You block phone numbers. You finish five bottles of red a week. You do. Thank you.

NHS recommendations

Apply a cool apology to the problem area immediately after exercise.

Do not eat the conversation that has been left out, unrefrigerated, for three days.

Wear comfortable gendered shoes that are designed to support your society.

Husband

He rubs off on her.

Wherever he's held her, she finds purple launched like spilt watercolour across her hand, elbow, the small of her back.

He enjoys winding his arm around her waist and gripping her hip as they walk. The mottled grey he leaves are confused capillaries.

She doesn't say anything, but she dislikes the way he always stands behind her chair in the company of dinner guests and owns her shoulders with his hands. He squeezes when he hopes a joke will land, then lets go when it does. It's not hard enough to hurt, but the marks left there are blunt straps of a rucksack, or something else insecure — a luggage she is unsure is hers.

When they argue, they stand on opposite sides of the bed. She sees it blossom from his chest like a delicate, bruised mushroom.

When she forgives him, he likes to peck her on the forehead like a child who's misbehaved and said sorry. She doesn't ask him to, but he takes the liberty of wiping her tear away with his thumb. When he does, her eye is smudged purple.

Pre-operative assessment

On a scale from grey to red, how much trouble does your hip give you when you a) walk up and down the stairs b) perform day-to-day activities e.g. laundry, shopping, showering c) perform low- to moderate-intensity sports? If yellow or below please proceed to next page. Do you have high blood pressure? Well-controlled? Not well-controlled? Please give details. Do you take aspirin regularly? Do you smoke tobacco of any kind e.g. cigarettes, cigars, pipes. Specify number per day. Do you experience blue? If so, please specify shade. How often do you feel orange? Insomnia? Yes. No. Not sure. Do you consume alcohol? If yes, how many units per week? Have you ever suffered from blood clots in the lungs or legs? Blackouts/faints? What shade of blue is your heart problem? Have you ever been treated for sickle cell anaemia? For spring green? Have you had a blood transfusion within the last 3 months? Do you have any personal or religious reasons for refusing to have any blood products given to you? Do you have/have you had memory problems or confusion? Woken at night with extreme breathlessness? Woken at night with extreme yellow? A history of acute confusion after an operation? A history of crying in your bed after an operation? Dizziness? Epilepsy or convulsions? Please add details here. Have you had serious problems following an anaesthetic? Specify. When discharged, do you have a responsible adult to drive you home following your surgery? Do you manage to brush your teeth every night with help, on your own with difficulty, on your own easily? Do you have someone available to stay with you overnight and help care for you? Do you have someone to stay with you overnight? Do you have someone? To stay? And sienna? And jade? And you experience 7 blues every day, and there is a 5% risk of temporary nerve damage due to distraction of the joint from the socket, and a 0.05% chance of permanent nerve damage, dead-foot, and loss of sensation in operated area, and you haven't thrown away her toothbrush, still, it's there in your bathroom cabinet, and your heart problems are green, and you've kept a birthday present for her under your bed, just in case you're talking by then, and you are required to avoid long-haul flights six weeks before and after operation to reduce the risk of blood clots, and please list any surgeries or minor procedures using anaesthetic you have had in the past year, and any other upcoming procedures and when are they scheduled? And how long was it since your last major surgery, and she's not going to be here this time, the way she was there the last time, when you woke up wearing a sick bowl, and you were still just getting to know each other but she sent you a text anyway, it said 'Thinking of you', and you were dizzy when you looked at screens, but when you read that, it fixed everything, and do you have a problem lying flat for at least 30 minutes because of difficulty breathing? And list all the medications you take, and blue, and blue, and you want to say that you're purple too, somewhere, and do you have any other illnesses, limitations or concerns we should know about?

Graduate

It licks up as turquoise
from the underside of your bed,
but you have put this behind you,
so you take your pillow and duvet
and sleep on the couch.

In the morning it curls through the window
of the kitchen, so you leave early.

It circles into the back of the cinema,
so you sit at the front.

You leave the nightclub before 12am
because you can't be sure
whether that pale creeping cloud is turquoise
or the smoke machine.

And when you get home,
it licks up from the underside of your bed.

The next day, it swells
into your rearview mirror,
a tsunami loading on the horizon
like lungs about to blow

put the pedal down

you've put it all behind you

you escape down the dual carriageway.

At the gym, you look over your shoulder.
There it is, leaking from the changing rooms
getting closer,
always closer.

You grasp at a button on the treadmill
and run faster.

You've probably never heard of it

lemonchiffon - *#fffacd*

    the exact point on a cheesecake when topping becomes cream; the delicate balance of gratefulness and resentment e.g. when the Subway staff member kindly fills up your Carbonara Pot Pasta with hot water without charging you anything, but puts too much hot water in it, way over the fill line, idiot, and now it's diluted and they've ruined it. They've ruined. It.

chartreuse - *#7fff00*

    you'll be forgiven for thinking it's green; but don't be fooled. Think excited Frankenstein. Think electrified frog. Think how a blade of grass would look when it's having an epiphany.

coquelicot - *#ff3800*

    the thinking man's red; the feeling when everyone else finds something funny, and you don't; the shade of a wedgie.

chamoisee - *#a0785a*

    brown ... with a history; brown ... with a story still to tell; an undernourished brown that grew up without a male role model; the pigment of yearning to be whole.

cinereous - *#98817b*

to the untrained eye ... grey. The shade of office blocks; of pain that is taller and more organised than you are. The hunch that your pain has more of a right to be here than you do.

cerulean - *#2a52be*

blue, but, like, so deep, you might not get it.

fulvous - *#e48400*

if SunnyD was alcoholic; intense. Earnest. That moment when the person you're arguing with down the phone has finally stopped interrupting you and is letting you say your piece and my god they're finally hearing you out and then you realise it's because they hung up.

smaragdine - *#01d758*

the shade of a surgeon's gown between anaesthetised eyelashes; the colour of constipation.

eburnean - *#750000*

if elephant tusks had feelings.

phlox - *#df00ff*

not like other pinks you've met.

purpureus - *#9a4eae*

purple's long-awaited sequel; its sophomore effort; the pain of dairy milk; one that sits in your fridge; that you grab at, at night, but resist during the day.

Colouring books are good for therapeutic purposes

You colour the sky green.
You colour the clouds brown.
You colour the cows orange.
You colour the grass yellow.
You make the people blue.

You are hungry after mealtimes.
You are lonely after hugs.
Being hit was the best thing
that ever happened to you.
Your graduation was the worst
day of your life.

The grapes in your fridge turn white.
You let the bread go pink.
You turn your birthday grey
because you make the people blue.

You sit in the garden when it rains.
You draw the curtains when it's sunny.
Your make the house black.
You turn your eye purple.
You colour your arms red.

You make the people blue.

For reference 2.0

Sitting in the clinic alone is typically blue,
the same as waiting three days for a WhatsApp reply

Finding the perfect prom dress is the same shade of apricot
as a 45-year-old man with a butt-crack leering at you over his
shoulder in Costa

Finding out you got into that university
is the same purple in your stomach when you step onto a
rowboat

The tenderness you feel when you say 'I do'
is the same pink as early-stage arthritis

Celebrating your three-year anniversary
is the same glow of orange when sleeping in a burning house

Eight-year-old

You left your watch on the boat. The silence
is crushing. Your father has the keys. He takes
you back to find it. Your mother and sister continue.
This is the fifth time you've disappointed him this holiday.

It is only a couple of turns through the harbour,
but it's just the two of you now, and enough time
for him to turn to you and say with precision,
like the doctor he is,
                                    'You stink'.

As you buckle the rainbow strap, check
the yellow face is smiling the right way up,
say 'Yes, Dad' when he asks for a reply,
you notice a tint in the air. Just a tinge.

It hangs about like an aroma
all the way through to your 10th birthday,
then to your 11th, then to your 12th.
You can't tell if other people notice;

you'd be so embarrassed if they did.
It lasts until the divorce. Then it's there
on your weekend visits. He pleads with you —
you see him so rarely; you've forgotten why,

but you can't shake the instinct of holding your breath
whenever you are alone with him.

In your graduation photo,
the family are finally back together again
for one proud moment.
But it's sepia, like a stench.

Granddaughter

Mum wakes you at 5 am. They got the call
from Queen Elizabeth's. She's gone.

You get dressed. Realise your grief
isn't in the room.

Open the wardrobe.
Not in here.

Shovel open the sock drawer.
Not even a dust cloud.

No puffs of colour from the legs of your denim,
no hints of air from your jacket pockets.

Switch the lights on. Check under the bed, between the folds
of the curtains.
Not even a little mist? Pale-cream? Goddamn tope? Well, fuck.

You think ahead to the hospital room. To the funeral.
Tagging onto crowds to hide your true colours

or more, the fact you have none.

Phrasebook. Non-exhaustive.

honeydew - *#f0fff0*
110 hrtz

'You okay?'

darkslategrey - *#2f4f4f*
317 hrtz

'Tea?'

aliceblue - *#f0f8ff*
945 hrtz

'Netflix?'

lightcoral - *#f08080*
1,004 hrtz

'You okay?'

lightseagreen - *#20b2aa*
1,324 hrtz

'Cheeky Nando's?'

peachpuff - *#ffdab9*
1,451 hrtz

'Cabernet sauvignon?'

papayawhip - *#ffefd5*
6,899 hrtz

'Ibiza with the lads?'

cornsilk - *#fff8dc*
13,923 hrtz

'Sure you okay?'

mistyrose - *#ffe4e1*
24,426 hrtz

'You'll be okay.'

mediumorchid - *#ba55d3*
47,998 hrtz

'You're okay.'

olivedrab - *#6b8e23*
99,833 hrtz

'Now that's a bit dramatic.'

dodgerblue - *#1e90ff*	'See someone?'
104,556 hrtz	
dimgrey - *#696969*	'Beta blockers?'
122,333 hrtz	
deepskyblue - *#00bfff*	'Fluoxetine?'
355,989 hrtz	
burlywood - *#deb887*	'Effexor 75 mg?'
406,245 hrtz	
snow - *#fffafa*	'Effexor 225 mg?'
554,329 hrtz	
steelblue - *#4682b4*	'Chlorpromanzine?'
657,889 hrtz	
thistle - *#d8bfd8*	'Relationship with father?'
809,768 hrtz	
sandybrown - *#f4a460*	'Relationship with chlorpromanzine?'
999,999 hrtz	
darkred - *#8b0000*	'Relationship with Netflix?'
1,009,898 hrtz	
whitesmoke - *#f5f5f5*	'You're going to be okay.'
1,107,334 hrtz	
seashell - *#fff5ee*	'Tea.'
1,306,339 hrtz	

Gender reveal

They hang azure paper garlands from the kitchen beam.
The balloons that frame the photo booth are cyan.

The wrapping tissue of your gifts is navy,
and inside lie tiny denim dungarees.

They take each bag of marshmallows and separate the blue
from the pink ones, and then they throw the pink ones away.

People put hands on your mother's belly
and cannot see the colours to come.

Better

And they hold doors open for you
and they stand up for you on trains
and they carry your drink because
your hands are busy with the crutches
and they ask about the stitches,
the keyholes the surgeon made
and will the sutures dissolve?
And have you been to the nurse yet
to get them removed?
And they see you struggle out of cars
and they pick you up and drop you off
and oh sorry, did that hurt?
And are you getting better?
And at night, alone in your bedroom,
you check beneath the bandage—
not the one they know about,
from the surgery —
but the other one.
It's not a wound.
It's a patch of purple.
It's something you've had all along.
It is not closing up.
And they hear you've started physio
and how are your exercises?
And are you sure you don't
need help with that stretch?
And will the stitches leave a scar?
And you pick up the crutches and drop them
and they give you a lift to hydrotherapy
and they pull up chairs for you
and before you sleep you slick
back the dressing —

the one no one knows you have.
It is the part of you that is wrong.
You think it is the reason why
you do things. You tinker with her.
You do not call him back. You snap at them
and the skin around it is getting angry.
And they notice you're on one crutch now
and are you fully weight-bearing soon?
And I see you're not wearing
the pressure socks anymore
and this time when you check,
the gauze does not stay on
it slides
because the wound is wet
like eyes
and they invite you on nights out now
and how does it feel to be walking again?
And it's the gym every day is it?
And I see you're moving faster now
and how long until you can run
and the wound is wet
and you pick her up and you drop her
all she wants to do is heal
and you pick her up and you drop her
and it is black now. It yawns.
It is bigger. It is you.
And they ask you
are you getting better?

For reference 3.0

The bright red of a customer sticking his finger in my face
and saying 'You're Chinese aren't you' can't be equal
to that moment in the changing rooms when Amy
stretched her eyelids to imitate me
but maybe if it happens seven times, it is.

You wouldn't think that hearing my parents
shout through the floorboards is equal
to that of being groped on the dance floor.
But then, I was told neither was my fault.
I just can't be sure.

And so far as you and I go,
it's quite clear that...

I swear though that the way I hurt you
was not deserving of the way you hurt me
but maybe if I did it seven times, it is.

And does that other time I hurt you
cancel out the other time you hurt me?
But then I was told neither was my fault
and I know they both were.

The purple I'm feeling right now,
it cannot compare to the amber you've gone through.

I know that.
I think.

Is mine...
is it...
is that enough?

Meanwhile

As a triage nurse cuts her eyes from you
to the colour chart on her clipboard.

As you sit across the desk from your project manager
and wonder if he is seeing your pain, or just looking at it.

As a graduate scheme candidate combs in her orange
so it blends with her hair before the interview.

As a couple tuck into linguine and mahogany
converges over their table.

There's tell of other places where pain isn't
translated into colours but sounds.

They say that, over there, the pavements are carpeted
with a hum. They wear hearing aids, not lenses.

They say that, over there, the first stage of grief sounds like
a string orchestra tuning its instruments before the first piece.

They say that, over there, ambulances wail high when rushing
to natural disasters and low for man-made.

They say that, over there, terror is a bass so low
it sounds like an explosion.

They say that if you carry your baby in a lifeboat, in vans,
in backs of trucks, over miles, your fear singing through octaves,

throbbing in quavers, news reporters from other countries
will trip you up as you run, to see what colour you'll bleed.

Natural phenomena

Are you watching a dazzling sunset
or your heart sink over the horizon?

Is that a rainbow
or your regret bending over the sky?

Is it a foggy morning
or can you not see through your grief today?

Are you taking a photo of the northern lights
or is that your loneliness writhing overhead?

Is it really an overcast day
or is that just your self-loathing blocking the sun?

Walk into it.

ACKNOWLEDGEMENTS:

To Stuart Bartholomew for making this pamphlet possible. I've put
you through a fair bit of orange, and probably a little bit of ochre too.
Thank you for your patience, your vision and your magic.

To Sean Colletti, the best editor I could have hoped for. Your
guidance, wisdom and friendship made all the difference.

If the International Hurtz Scale did flatmates, they would run from
1 to Hazel Sealeaf. Thank you for your generosity of heart, and the
hours spent chatting in our lounge.

To Bethany Slinn, whose excitement for life, love of art and personal
encouragement was crucial for this pamphlet to exist.

To Leon, whose belief in me makes me always want to push further.

To Mum, Dad, Gabby. Because of you three, I can do anything.

To Bohdan Piasecki for your life-changing advice and support. To
Luke Kennard for your kind words. To Jacob Sam-La Rose for your
ongoing inspiration.

To Jack Crowe, Kamil Mahmood and Abi Budgen for your time
looking at extracts of *Hurtz*, and willingness to answer my
many, many questions.

To Jade, Afiya and my other friends outside of poetry. For all
you know, I could be a terrible poet, but you're cheering me on
anyway.

To the incredible individuals in the spoken word community, in
Birmingham and beyond. You've each made me who I am, and
I do it for all of you.

ABOUT THE AUTHOR:

Jasmine Gardosi is a previous BBC Arts Young Creative and Poet-in-Residence for the Shakespeare Birthplace Trust. A multiple slam champion, she has been shortlisted for Birmingham Poet Laureate and the Out-Spoken Prize for Poetry. She has appeared on BBC Radio 3's *The Verb*, BBC Asian Network and at Glastonbury Festival. Her work has been featured globally by Standard Chartered for their International Women's Day campaign, and recently through Button Poetry, the world's largest spoken word platform, after being awarded an Honourable Mention for Outstanding International Entry in their 2018 video contest. A Ledbury Poetry Festival board member, she runs West Midlands Poets' Place and co-facilitates the Hippodrome Young Poets.

ABOUT VERVE POETRY PRESS

Verve Poetry Press is a new press focussing intently on meeting a local need in Birmingham - a need for the vibrant poetry scene here in Brum to find a way to present itself to the poetry world via publication. Co-founded by Stuart Bartholomew and Amerah Saleh, it is publishing poets from all corners of the city - poets that represent the city's varied and energetic qualities and will communicate its many poetic stories.

Added to this is an experimental and spoken pamphlet series featuring poets who have previously performed at the festival, and a debut performance poetry series, which will see us working with the brightest rising stars on the UK spoken word scene.

Like the festival, we will strive to think about poetry in inclusive ways and embrace the multiplicity of approaches towards this glorious art.

www.vervepoetrypress.com
@VervePoetryPres
mail@vervepoetrypress.com